D1566236

1

Christian Medical & Dental Associations
P.O. Box 7500
Bristol, TN 37621

World Wide Web: www.cmda.org
E-mail: main@cmda.org

Cover designed by PLOW Studio

Unless otherwise identified, all Scripture quotations are taken from The Holy Bible,
English Standard Version® (ESV®), Copyright © 2001 by Crossway, a publishing ministry
of Good News Publishers. All rights reserved. ESV Text Edition: 2007

ISBN 978-0-9897598-0-9

LCCN 2013952160

Printed in the United States of America

A MISSIONAL LIFE

A life surrendered
to Christ for service
in line with the
Great Commission,
following wherever
and however that may
unfold. Marked by

a deep commitment
and obedience
governed by a close
relationship with Christ
to closely listen,
continually hear,
and follow through.

TABLE OF
CONTENTS

1 | **IT'S A LIFESTYLE** | Florence Muindi | **10**

2 | **MOTIVATION MATTERS** | Brian Vickers | **16**

3 | **MISSIONS-MINDED EDUCATIONAL PLANNING** | Jeff Lewis | **22**

4 | **PATHWAYS TO FULL-TIME INTERNATIONAL MISSIONS** | John McVay | **28**

5 | **A BIBLICAL PERSPECTIVE** | Brian Fikkert | **34**

6 | **MENTORING** | Will Rogers | **40**

7 | **IT STARTS LOCALLY** | Rick Donlon | **46**

8 | **SELECTING A SHORT-TERM TRIP** | Don Thompson | **52**

9 | **NAVIGATING SENDING AGENCIES** | Scott Reichenbach | **58**

10 | **BUILDING A FINANCIAL PLAN** | Rick Allen | **66**

11 | **OVERCOMING CHALLENGES TO MISSIONS** | David Stevens | **72**

12 | **UNDERSTANDING CURRENT HEALTHCARE NEEDS** | Clydette Powell | **78**

13 | **THE FUTURE OF MISSIONS** | Gil Odendaal | **88**

14 | **PRAYING THROUGH MISSIONS PREPARATION** | Geneva Oaks | **94**

WHY DID WE WRITE THIS BOOK?

Engaging in the story the Lord is shaping around us is
a challenge, but also a wonderful invitation. I fully believe
the Lord allows and even plans for these challenges
so our character grows stronger and our hearts find
their definition in Him. I also believe the challenges are
opportunities for us as a community to develop solutions,
experience the blessing of working together,
and grow in faith as we wrestle through them.

THERE'S NO REASON TO FEEL ALONE,
and that's our purpose with this book.

HOW IS THIS BOOK BUILT?

It might sound like a negative starting point, but we began by trying to identify the major obstacles to engaging in missions. We listened to hundreds of individuals and organizations, compiled list after list, and finally narrowed it down to a dozen or more major obstacles that seem to draw the most attention.

Once we had identified the major points of discussion, we began planning how to address each one. We believed the best way was to bring together the full community of leaders in medical missions and allow the experts to speak to each respective area. Why not have a resource for the community created by the community?

And so the quest began. We developed a chapter-by-chapter plan and considered who might best speak into each of these areas. Each author was asked to contribute a short chapter on the specified topic within the context of our predefined goal for that chapter. We also accumulated resources and other recommendations. The goal was simple: to dig into the point quickly and precisely, to provide tangible resources and relevant wisdom, and to ease the tension that our hearts feel around each subject.

Once we had the content from these leaders, we began to build an engaging graphic style. We wanted something that didn't feel like a book, but more of a companion. We wanted a tool that could easily draw out discussions with mentors. We wanted a book that felt like you were having a conversation with a friend.

WHO IS THIS BOOK FOR?

Well, everyone! Most specifically, it's for those trying to discover what a pathway to missions looks like. But we aren't trying to "make" missionaries out of you. Missions isn't something you do. Missions is a way of life. So our greatest goal in this project is to see you living a more missional life. We want to create a conversation about how you are handling that piece of the Lord's call on your life.

HOW SHOULD I READ THIS BOOK?

Start by reading the book by yourself, then read it together with some friends. The topics are intentional and they will no doubt draw up feelings and emotions that are worth unpacking with others. You may want to have your parents, spouse, girlfriend/boyfriend, friends, or others close to you read through the book as well, especially if you've had a difficult time talking with them about some of these topics.

But when it's all said and done, just remember you are not alone. We are all on this journey together, walking together, learning together, and sharing together. Remember the obstacles are exciting, as they give you rich opportunity to trust in the Lord. And remember that there is great joy in a missional life, one filled with His pleasure as you seek His glory.

Blessings to you on your journey—it's a unique path just as unique as you are, and it's worth the fight.

Soli Deo Gloria!

Will Rogers

IT'S A
LIFESTYLE

by
Florence Muindi, M.D.

MISSIONS IS A LIFESTYLE, NOT A THING YOU DO.

THIS IS WHO YOU ARE.

THIS IS WHO YOU ARE.

 aul says, "It is no longer I who lives but Christ lives in me." Literally he had come to a place where he allowed God to own his life. He submitted to God's desires and gave up the right to have his way. He existed to serve his Father's will and did not live for any ambition, career, or plan that served himself or anyone else. He lived to represent God, and God's will for him was his life.

A missional life is not "settling" or losing passion—quite the opposite! It means setting aside your dreams to take up something grander. It means becoming so consumed that it becomes your life and reason for living. In due time it becomes a God-sized adventure as you see what He sees and learn to soar in faith. It means allowing yourself to be spent for something that has eternal value.

God allows us many ways to interact with His Kingdom. We can be in charge, making every effort to reach a desired destination on our own, or we can pursue Him, love Him, and follow Him where He leads. It's a very active surrender—that's what makes it an adventure.

Our surrender is for His service, which is counter to the secular world. It does not line up with the world's measures of success. In this pursuit, we may stay right where we are, or be called to go to another place. Either way, it's always against self and the against the norm.

The mission He invites us to is clear: Make disciples. We find ourselves in a position where we can call others to follow us as we follow Christ, in our everyday life, and in our spiritual actions. We learn from Him and model it for others as we obey and set an example for others to emulate. We serve Him on his commissioning terms. It takes commitment not to delay when He calls or compromise when He directs. We know His unfolding will when we abide in Him by the practice of prayer and reading the Word, walking hand-in-hand with God and in fellowship with His church.

A MISSIONAL LIFE
REQUIRES COMMITMENT,
NOT A SET DESTINATION OR A PARTICULAR ACCOMPLISHMENT.

This lifestyle of obedience may be marked with sacrifice. It may be in the workplace, in a distant country, or right in our homes. It fulfills His commissioning for the body of Christ and also at a very personal level.

It grows to the point where the effort is not on a conscious level.

IT BECOMES THE LIFE WE LEAD AND WE WOULD NOT OPT FOR ANOTHER.

I came to this kind of surrender many years after I had committed my life to Christ. I had not yet allowed God to own me and then I came to understand that His work required a living sacrifice. So I entered into covenant allowing Him to own me. I brought an end to my dreams and ushered in His will. I committed to seek Him with the full intention of obeying Him, no matter what that might look like. I embarked on a lifelong journey, pursuing Him and His purpose.

God may not show us what is to come, but He gives us enough information to follow. Obedience and continued obedience to what is revealed keep opening the next chapter. It would be overwhelming if He showed us the full measure of His will for us in advance.

After that initial surrender, His will became my life and I pursued Him with my all. He led me into medical school, marriage, further studies, children, cross-cultural missions, and the founding of an organization. He caused the work to grow through partnerships and programs in several nations—declaring His glory and His marvelous deeds among His people. And it continues without consuming or burdening me. He is establishing His work through His people and I get to participate in what He is doing. The results cause others to gain life and purpose that will count in eternity.

Life in Abundance, our organization, has grown incredibly beyond what I could ever have imagined and in ways I could never have planned. It has brought me to a place where only God can sustain. He has a plan for me and it's not based on me. I am but a tool in His hand for the time He allows me to live.

Dr. Florence Muindi is considered a thought leader in the ministry of community development. She is the founding president/CEO of Life In Abundance International, an African-founded, faith-based community development organization serving in 10 countries throughout Africa and the Caribbean.

A native to Kenya, Dr. Muindi has pioneered LIA's transformational development model, which empowers the church to meet the needs of the most vulnerable. She speaks at various international forums and churches on the use of health in partnership with churches to advance the Kingdom.

She is a graduate of University Of Nairobi Medical School and holds an MD. Additionally, she has a Masters in Public Health, as well as a diploma in Urban Poor Theology from Fuller Seminary.

She is married to Festus and they have two grown sons. Above all, Dr. Muindi is a servant and follower of Christ, fulfilling the Great Commission.

IS YOUR LIFE SURRENDERED TO CHRIST?

Was there a moment where you gave Him that complete control?
Is He still in charge today?

Are you committed to service? **Are you giving your life away for something that is not self-serving, but is a living sacrifice so that others may know and have life?**

As the journey unfolds, are you following without procrastination or compromise?

Are difficulties or sin holding you back?

Are blessings distracting you from moving on to the next season?

Listening to the still small voice is intentional. Listening with your heart and knowing when it's not right is key, as is guarding your heart to remain pure. **A CALLOUSED AND DISLOYAL HEART WILL NOT DO.** Is the Lord creating a clean heart and renewing a right spirit in you manifested by a sweet attitude and the flow of his presence?

He invites us to finish well.

Are we keeping on in the race?
Are we staying focused on Christ and on pleasing Him alone?

CONSIDER
THESE QUESTIONS

Have you lost the passion and commitment you displayed when you first began? Have you become passive and lethargic? Are you committed to pursuing excellence and maximum returns for the Kingdom?

A MISSIONAL LIFE IS GOVERNED BY A CLOSE RELATIONSHIP WITH CHRIST.

Are you investing in that relationship, taking time to talk and spend time alone with Christ? Is activity stealing that relationship?

We serve on His terms as outlined in His Word and in line with His commissioning.

ARE YOU COMMISSIONED AND STAYING ON COURSE WITH WHAT HE HAS INSTRUCTED?

Have you stagnated in what you heard years ago and become dogmatic?

ARE YOU OPEN TO THE CONTINUAL TEACHING OF GOD'S SPIRIT?

Is His Word still alive in you to inspire, correct, and train you in righteousness?

DISOBEDIENCE CAN CAUSE DISQUALIFICATION.

It cost Saul the kingship. Are you living in obedience daily?
Is that delayed in some areas of your life? Does your conscience convict you?

MOTIVATION
MATTERS

by
Brian Vickers, M.A., M.Div., Ph.D.

BIBLICAL RESPONSIBILITY

SOCIAL RESPONSIBILITY

There is an increased social conscience in this generation of Christians. Recognizing the shortcomings in the past, and wanting to do more, many want to address suffering of various kinds and fight it. This desire is well-intentioned, but is it always well-motivated? **How should we, as Christians, think about our responsibility in the world?** It's a huge question, and too big to fully answer here, but we can ask a few vital questions to put our mission in this world in biblical perspective.

QUESTIONS TO ASK:

Do we find ourselves motivated primarily by perceived weaknesses
in the Church, and ineffective work done by "other Christians,"
or are we motivated primarily by God's call on our life through
Christ as revealed in the Bible?

Are we motivated by a general need to "do something" or do
we desire to see the knowledge of God's glory cover the earth,
"as the waters cover the sea." (Habakkuk 2:14)?

How we answer these kinds of questions will largely determine whether we are
focused on being disciples of Christ acting on his behalf for the good of others, or
merely reacting and rebelling; whether we are truly missional or merely have a
social conscience; whether we are living for Christ or for ourselves.

What motivates us matters. It's easy to point back to the failures of generations
past—just like, believe it or not, it will be easy for the next generation to point
back at our shortcomings. It's easy to think about the suffering "out there" and
talk about what the Church doesn't do to alleviate it. What's challenging, difficult,
and thrilling beyond words is to catch a vision of what the Bible has to say about
our place in this world as ambassadors of Christ the King, confronted every day
with people made in His image, with the privilege of living for the sake of God and
others instead of ourselves, and to look at every day as connected to God's eternal
plan to redeem his people and the world we live in.

My missional life was started almost by "accident." Several years ago I was asked to consider being a faculty team leader on a student trip to South Asia. The original team leader was unable to go and if a new leader wasn't found, the trip was off. I had been to Europe, lived in England for a time, and visited a couple places in Africa, but I had never been to Asia. It sounded like a good idea, and something of an adventure, so I immediately said "yes!" Little did I know that what started that day as really just an exciting idea and potentially great experience—another notch on my travel belt—would be the door God opened to show me how great an opportunity he gives us to take part in the epic story of His mission in the world.

Of course I supported and promoted missions, but once I went—even short-term—I understood the difference between talking about missions (after all, it's in the Bible) and learning to live missionally whether abroad or at home. Now I am actively involved in leading frequent short-term trips, consulting others going on trips, teaching overseas, speaking and writing on missions, motivating and mobilizing "senders," and trying to live my life knowing that geography is only ever secondary, but faithfulness to Christ is primary, wherever I may be.

Over the years, being part of GMHC has been one of the major ways God has kept missions front and center in my life. Through GMHC, I've met all sorts of dear brothers and sisters I wouldn't have met otherwise, and heard stories and experiences that were as unimaginable as they were inspiring. Through it, my vision of the world and what God's people are doing in it expands year by year.

Dr. Vickers currently serves as the Assistant Editor of The Southern Baptist Journal of Theology. Dr. Vickers is actively involved in leading short-term mission trips and teaching overseas. He has written Jesus' Blood and Righteousness: Paul's Theology of Imputation, *and has published articles in* Trinity Journal, The Southern Baptist Journal of Theology, Eusebia, Gospel Witness, *and* The New Holman Bible Dictionary. *He is a member of* The Evangelical Theological Society *and* The Institute for Biblical Research.

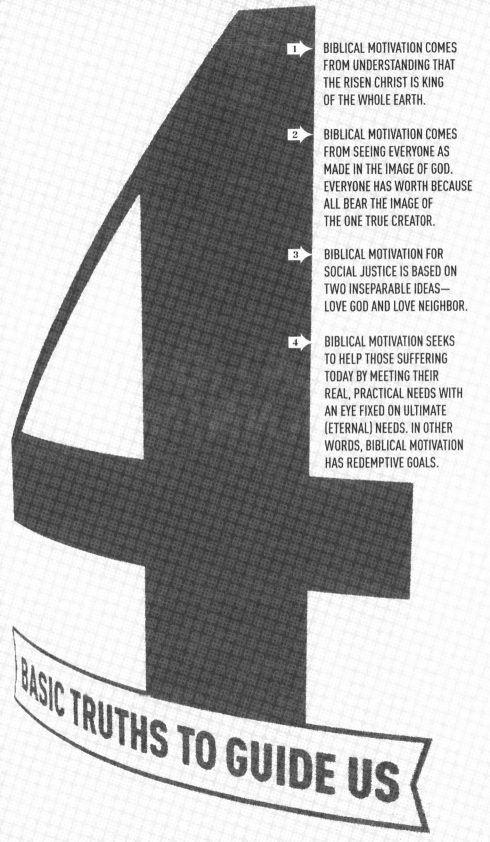

1 BIBLICAL MOTIVATION COMES FROM UNDERSTANDING THAT THE RISEN CHRIST IS KING OF THE WHOLE EARTH.

2 BIBLICAL MOTIVATION COMES FROM SEEING EVERYONE AS MADE IN THE IMAGE OF GOD. EVERYONE HAS WORTH BECAUSE ALL BEAR THE IMAGE OF THE ONE TRUE CREATOR.

3 BIBLICAL MOTIVATION FOR SOCIAL JUSTICE IS BASED ON TWO INSEPARABLE IDEAS— LOVE GOD AND LOVE NEIGHBOR.

4 BIBLICAL MOTIVATION SEEKS TO HELP THOSE SUFFERING TODAY BY MEETING THEIR REAL, PRACTICAL NEEDS WITH AN EYE FIXED ON ULTIMATE (ETERNAL) NEEDS. IN OTHER WORDS, BIBLICAL MOTIVATION HAS REDEMPTIVE GOALS.

4

BASIC TRUTHS TO GUIDE US

MISSIONS-MINDED
EDUCATIONAL
PLANNING

by
Jeffrey Lewis, R.Ph., Pharm.D., M.A.C.M

TAKING SIMPLE
EDUCATIONAL STEPS

GAINING REAL EXPERIENCE
IN THE PROCESS.

THE PHILOSOPHY

Education is not a "timeout" from life, a stage devoted simply to prepping for what's next. Education is a lifelong pursuit...a journey...something to be laid at the feet of Jesus in worship every day. At the conclusion of any formal level of education you will, undoubtedly, possess more knowledge and skills for life (missions and otherwise) than you had before. But you already have knowledge and skills from your life experiences to this point, and those things can and should be used now.

THE GOAL

The goal of education certainly includes gaining knowledge, and may include many disciplines—God can use everything on the mission field. But, more than knowledge, education is about developing life skills like communication, critical thinking and problem solving, data gathering, relationship development, time management, teamwork, leadership, self-discipline, and more. These are the things we use in every aspect of life...family, vocation, and ministry. Careers change often, and a well-developed set of life skills makes these transitions possible and helps you follow God wherever He leads. Do not simply pursue knowledge; use educational pursuits as opportunities to develop additional skills for life. Then, through the Spirit, ask God to add wisdom so you can serve Him well.

THE PROCESS

As you choose a school or post-graduate program, consider how your experience at that institution will prepare you to serve. Consider the institution's mission and values. Is it faith-based (not imperative, but often advantageous)? Is it focused on serving others (and fostering the same in its students)? Is it focused on leadership (especially developing servant-leaders)? Join student organizations which have a similar focus. At each level of education, take advantage of experiences in school, in the church, and in the community, to further develop your skills. Take your classroom experience into the field and put it into action!

As you choose an area of study, consider how God has wired you. Ask your family, friends, and mentors for their thoughts; their insights are often clearer than our own. Take a career assessment. Don't be afraid to change direction as you gain insight into your aptitudes. In addition to your primary area of study, a missional life will be well-served by knowledge in many other areas.

THE FOCUS

As you consider your educational plan at any stage of the journey, keep this question in mind: "How am I going to serve?" The primary question is not "What am I going to be?" or "What am I going to do?" Our journey is about serving, and that includes our educational plans. In addition, remember that learning is an act of worship. It should, therefore, be pursued with all of your heart, mind, soul, and strength.

Jeffrey Lewis

My educational journey has been fairly successful—in the world's eyes. Classroom success and associated honors accompanied my secondary, undergraduate (BS Pharmacy), and graduate (Doctor of Pharmacy) education; however, my focus was certainly not missional. My journey wasn't guided by "How can I serve?" but "How can I be respected and provide for myself and my family?"

I managed to acquire some helpful tools for missions along the way—a license to practice pharmacy, some limited foreign language training, and skills in time management, leadership, communication, and personal financial management. But as I began my fourth decade of life, intentional preparation for service captured my heart. The pursuit of a master's degree in Christian Ministries and a construction-focused mission trip to Costa Rica (both at God's nudging) altered my focus and revealed the extent to which I had failed to maximize previous educational opportunities for effective service.

I have attempted to be more strategic in my pursuits since that time, and God has brought a number of colleagues, friends, mentors, and professional and personal opportunities to support my development.

My present role at Cedarville University is focused on helping pharmacy students do what I wish had marked my own life at their stage in the journey—thinking about their education as an act of worship and preparing to serve in the most effective way possible. Whether it's in the classroom, at the local coffee shop, or in a Guatemalan medical clinic, it's my privilege to assist the next generation in the pursuit of a missional life. I continue to learn (it's a lifelong process, remember?) and am grateful that our Lord is patient and full of grace.

Dr. Lewis received his Bachelor of Science in Pharmacy from Ohio Northern University and Doctor of Pharmacy from the University of Cincinnati. After completing a specialized residency in hospital pharmacy administration at the Medical College of Virginia Hospitals, he returned to his home state of Ohio to assume the role of Clinical Coordinator at Timken Mercy Medical Center in Canton, and subsequently the Manager of Clinical Pharmacy Services at Summa Health System in Akron. While in these roles, Dr. Lewis was responsible for developing and maintaining many of the systems and processes that affect quality institutional drug use (e.g. formulary management, hospital staff education, Continuous Quality Improvement efforts related to safe medication use). Through this work he developed a special interest and expertise in medication error reduction strategies.

"For the Lord gives wisdom;
from his mouth come
knowledge and understanding;
for wisdom will come
into your heart, and
knowledge will be
pleasant to your soul;"

Proverbs 2:6, 10

Resources and References

Websites
www.careerdirectonline.com
www.cccu.org
www.CrossroadCareer.org
www.intervarsity.org

PATHWAYS TO FULL-TIME
INTERNATIONAL MISSIONS

by

John McVay, M.Div.

EXPLORING PRACTICAL NEXT STEPS AT WHATEVER STAGE OF PREPARATION YOU ARE IN.

After his conversion to Christ, the Apostle Paul

HOW DID GOD PREPARE

had a training season of 13 years,

THE FIRST MISSIONARY?

including mentoring from Barnabas.

While pathways into full-time missions vary,
steps include the following:

PERSONAL SPIRITUAL FORMATION

Become grounded in scripture and in prayer. Develop the lifestyle of a daily quiet time. In the ambiguity and stress of another culture, past experience and events too often shape reactions. Instead, let the Lord transform you. Then you can say, "Yes, I've been through past trials. I know God can bring me through this struggle and future trials as well."

Many problems missionaries have involve relationships. Be humble. Learn to serve under authority, at church, at school, and at a job. How faithful and teachable are you? How do you handle confrontation? How do you deal with bitterness?

DISCOVER YOUR MINISTRY GIFTING

In addition to your profession, try two, three, or four ministries. Don't just stay in one role for years. Let others say, "Yes, you're really good at this," or "You think you're gifted at that, but you're not."

You can express your *willingness* to serve. And you can trust God to confirm *His* plans for you.

EDUCATION

You need a solid foundation in understanding the Bible, missions, and the world. An excellent way to learn the Bible is by teaching a class or leading a Bible study.

Take the course Perspectives on the World Christian Movement, which is available in most cities or online. Encourage yourself through reading missionary biographies. Find a mentor. Read the Operation World prayer guide and use it to intercede for the unreached.

EXPOSURE TO OTHER CULTURES

The ability to understand and accept others is essential. Start now by befriending an international student. In most cities there are hundreds of students from foreign countries. Tragically, most never hear the gospel.

Participate in a short-term outreach. One purpose is to find your place. If God does not later lead you into full-time service, you will be better equipped to be a "sender" and lifetime supporter.

CONNECT WITH A SENDING AGENCY

The Apostle Paul always took others with him as part of the missionary team. Before selecting another short-term trip or missions training, explore what agency God may have you join. Ask what kind of short-term experience or training they recommend.

PRAY

Are you praying more for God's will for you than for His kingdom to come on earth as it is in heaven?

Pray, not just for your part, but for God's will to be done through whomever He chooses. It is His harvest and we are His workers.

The longer the preparation, the greater the role God can develop.

Time spent sharpening the ax is not time wasted.

Be open to all the preparation the Lord desires.

Several months after my wife and I began as full-time missionaries, we wrote our sending agency the following message:

"Mission Control, we have a problem. We wish we could say that it is only in the movies, but the likelihood of meltdown here is increasing. Two members of our family are adjusting poorly. Our relationships with non-Christians are progressing slowly. Our children have been stressed in school and it is quite difficult to help them with homework at our low level of language proficiency. Another missionary has been a terrific support for us and for our kids but he is leaving next month. We've learned much about the culture and how hard it is to be here. Our limited facility in the language is a daily frustration and we are weary of the frequent criticism and absence of encouragement that is so typical in this culture."

Serving as a full-time term missionary can be a huge challenge. During our darkest days I would read Hebrews 11 aloud twice a day and pray for the faith to keep going. One day I continued into the next chapter and read Hebrews 12:11: "For the moment all discipline seems painful rather than pleasant...." I wondered if the Lord was disciplining me. Had I been disobedient? Then I read Hebrews 12:7: "It is for discipline that you have to endure. God is treating you as sons. For what son is there whom his father does not discipline?" Then I saw it. The hardship is something God brought into my life. I reread verse 11 and exchanged the word discipline for hardship. "For the moment all hardship seems painful rather than pleasant, but later it yields the peaceful fruit of righteousness to those who have been trained by it."

We persevered and God brought breakthroughs. And we were grateful we did not skip any preparation God had for us before we came.

John McVay (M.Div) and his wife Nicole (RN, MSNE) live in Tulsa where John serves as Chief of Staff for In His Image Family Medicine Residency and Medical Missions. John co-founded The Journey Deepens retreats for aspiring missionaries and AskAMissionary.com online Q&A. He also serves as Academic Dean of Missions Preparation for the Global Missions Health Conference.

Jesus takes us over for His enterprises, His building schemes entirely, and no soul has any right to claim where he shall be put.

— Oswald Chambers

Resources and References

Books
Global Mission Handbook
by Steve Hoke and Bill Taylor
Operation World
by Jason Mandryk
Missionary Biographies
by Janet and Geoff Benge
Christian Heroes: Hudson Taylor and others
by Janet and Geoff Benge
Experiencing God: Knowing and Doing His Will
(Workbook) by Henry Blackaby

Websites
www.medicalmissions.com
www.askamissionary.com
www.preparingtogo.com
www.missionnext.com
www.perspectives.org
www.thejourneydeepens.org

Experiences
Global Missions Health Conference
The Perspectives course
The Journey Deepens weekend retreats

CHAPTER
5

A BIBLICAL
PERSPECTIVE

by
Brian Fikkert, Ph.D.

ENGAGING IN MISSIONS
IN A MANNER THAT
DOESN'T STRIP THE
DIGNITY OF THOSE
WE SERVE OR MAKE THEM
DEPENDENT ON US.

oing missions in the Global South means doing missions among the poor. How will you respond to the homeless man on the streets of Mumbai, the shoeless orphan in a Cairo slum, or the hungry widow in Niger?

Our first impulse is to give these people what they are lacking: housing, shoes, and food. Although such a response may help in the short run, such handouts treat symptoms rather than underlying causes and can create crippling dependencies if prolonged. To be truly effective, we need to address the root causes of poverty, which are rooted in the grand drama of Scripture.

The first chapter of this grand drama reveals a relational God who creates human beings in His image, wiring us for relationship, as well—with God, self, others, and the rest of creation. When we experience these relationships in the way God intended, we experience humanness in its fullest sense.

Unfortunately, The Fall distorted each of these relationships, which leads to a profound truth: We are all poor in the sense that none of us experiences these relationships in the way God intended. Unless we embrace this truth—unless we acknowledge our own poverty—our work with the materially poor is likely to hurt them and ourselves. Let me explain...

Research has found that shame is often the way low-income people experience brokenness with self. Instead of seeing themselves as being created in the image of God, low-income people often feel they are inferior and are incapable of improving their situation. Although there are many factors that hinder them from making progress—including social injustice—these feelings of inferiority are often a major obstacle.

 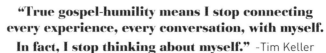

"True gospel-humility means I stop connecting every experience, every conversation, with myself. In fact, I stop thinking about myself." -Tim Keller

Those of us with higher incomes also experience brokenness with self, but rather than shame, our brokenness typically involves pride. We tend to believe that we have achieved our good fortune through our own efforts and that we are qualified to "play God" in the lives of the materially poor. As a result, the things that we do to help often communicate, "We are superior, and you need us to save you." Such an approach enhances their shame and our pride, making both of us more broken than ever before.

Fortunately, there is more to the grand drama: Jesus Christ is reconciling all things (Colossians 1:19-20). To "reconcile" means to put into right relationship again. Indeed, the good news of the gospel is that Jesus Christ is addressing the root causes of poverty by restoring all people—both materially poor and non-poor—to right relationship with God, self, others, and the rest of creation.

Yes, we must use our resources to help the materially poor, but our approach must be an empowering one that seeks to restore them to a sense of dignity, worth, and capacity, because "Colossians 1 Jesus" is about restoration. Surprisingly, the first step towards such restoration is repentance...our repentance, for we too are broken, and we too need to be restored.

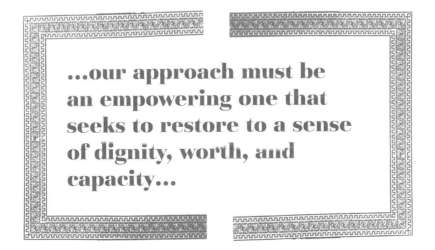

...our approach must be an empowering one that seeks to restore to a sense of dignity, worth, and capacity...

PERSONAL JOURNEY — Brian Fikkert

My commitment to poverty alleviation began in high school when I read Rich Christians in an Age of Hunger *by Ron Sider. This book convinced me that as a follower of Jesus Christ, I needed to care for poor people, and I devoted my life to this cause.*

Blessed with mathematical ability, I pursued a Ph.D. in economics, focusing on international economics and development. Upon the completion of my dissertation, many urged me to use my degree to teach at a Christian college. I vowed I would never do that, as I wanted to "play in the big leagues." So I took a job at the University of Maryland, just outside of Washington, D.C. I relished the idea of doing cutting-edge research at a major university and trying to work with global institutions such as the World Bank.

But God had a different plan. Over time, He made me increasingly uncomfortable with the basic assumptions, methodologies, tools, and prescriptions of much of mainstream economics. And as He did this, He called me to—you guessed it—a professorship at a very small Christian college where I could explore a distinctively Christian approach to poverty.

I went kicking and screaming, but God has blessed this move. He has used the entire Covenant College community—board, administration, professors, staff, and students— to help me come to a more biblical understanding of human beings, of poverty, of my own brokenness, and of God's work in the world. Their discipleship has helped me to understand God's redeeming story more deeply and to play a small role in the proclamation of His kingdom. It turns out that this is the "big leagues," not in the eyes of the world but in the eyes of "Colossians 1 Jesus," who is reconciling all things, including me.

Dr. Brian Fikkert is the Founder and Executive Director of the Chalmers Center for Economic Development at Covenant College, where he also serves as a Professor of Economics and Community Development. Brian received a Ph.D. in Economics with highest honors from Yale University and a B.A. in Mathematics from Dordt College. Specializing in Economic Development and International Economics, Brian has authored numerous academic and popular publications and is a co-author of the book When Helping Hurts: How to Alleviate Poverty without Hurting the Poor...and Yourself. *Prior to coming to Covenant College, he was a professor at the University of Maryland and a research fellow at the Center for Institutional Reform and the Informal Sector. Brian, his wife Jill, and his three children are honored to be members of New City Fellowship Presbyterian Church (PCA) in Chattanooga, TN.*

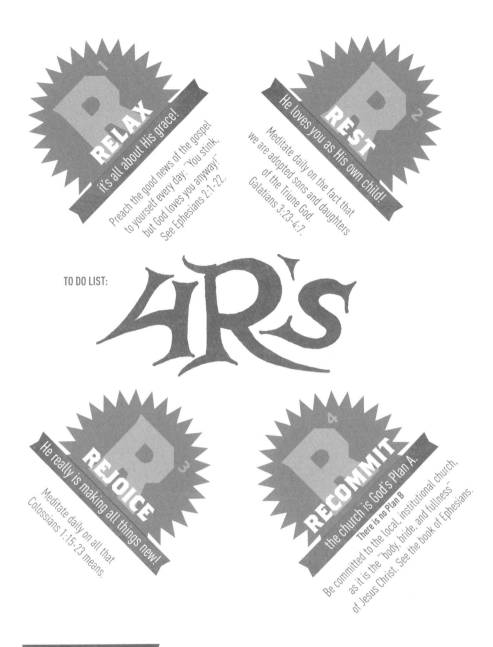

TO DO LIST: 4R's

R¹ RELAX
it's all about His grace!
Preach the good news of the gospel to yourself every day: "You stink, but God loves you anyway!" See Ephesians 2:1-22.

R² REST
He loves you as His own child!
Meditate daily on the fact that we are adopted sons and daughters of the Triune God. Galatians 3:23-4:7.

R³ REJOICE
He really is making all things new!
Meditate daily on all that Colossians 1:15-23 means.

R⁴ RECOMMIT
the church is God's Plan A. **There is no Plan B**
Be committed to the local, institutional church, as it is the "body, bride, and fullness." of Jesus Christ. See the book of Ephesians.

Resources and References

Books

When Helping Hurts: How to Alleviate Poverty without Hurting the Poor...and Yourself
by Steve Corbett and Brian Fikkert

To Live in Peace: Biblical Faith and the Changing Inner City
by Mark Gornik

Prodigal God
by Tim Keller

Walking With the Poor
by Bryant Myers

Let Justice Roll Down
by John Perkins

Rich Christians in an Age of Hunger: Moving from Affluence to Generosity
by Ron Sider

Websites

www.chalmers.org
www.whm.org/sonship

CHAPTER 6

MENTORING

by
Will Rogers

UNDERSTANDING
THE IMPORTANCE
OF MENTOR RELATIONSHIPS
AND HOW TO SIMPLY ENGAGE
WITH A MENTOR.

MENTORING

...doesn't that sound daunting?

It can be, for both the mentor and the person being mentored... but it shouldn't be!

The Lord has wired us to be relational and He intends for us to learn from one another.

Mentoring is a blessing, an opportunity to pass knowledge from one generation to another and preserve a rich heritage.

But the idea of mentoring has been largely lost in our culture and too often it's regarded with fear. Too many potential mentors believe they have to have it all "figured out" before they can be helpful, and too many of the people hoping to learn from a mentor believe they must find someone who's an expert in every area.

These myths keep many great relationships from beginning.

MICRO-MENTORING.

Rather than trying to find (or to be) a perfect mentor, start by assessing areas of your life where you could use someone's wisdom—perhaps with career decisions, financial planning, spiritual questions, or any sort of personal and relationship questions. Now what if you were to find different people, each knowledgeable in one of these areas, and ask if they would each meet with you a few times to unpack some thoughts and help you walk through some decisions?

If you want to be mentored, it's essential to pursue the mentor. You can't wait for the opportunity to come to you. Take the lead and clearly state the expectations. Tell the person you'd like to meet a few times (set a number) and you'd like to talk about a specific topic (something they are comfortable with). Give them a few examples of what you're wrestling through. You'll be hard-pressed to find someone who isn't willing to meet a few times to talk through an area of life where they have experience and expertise. The amazing thing about getting together with someone for a few set meetings is you're courting this person to see if this mentor might be someone with whom you could dig into other pieces of life, but without the pressure.

Facts and knowledge may be passed through books and classes, **but wisdom is passed through relationships and the Holy Spirit.** Mentoring relationships are essential for a healthy Christian life. So wherever you are, take the initiative. If you're a student then find a mentor. If you're a professional with any experience, you should be walking with someone younger to help her map a path in life. To all there is a call for being engaged in mentoring. This is our duty and our joy as believers, to share the many great lessons and wisdom the Lord has taught us.

I'll always remember Andy Stanley saying mentoring isn't about filling someone else's cup, but it's about emptying your own cup into someone else. Mentoring is not about making someone else full, it's about fully pouring yourself out.

Will Rogers

My first exposure to this idea of a missional life was while on a Boy Scout trip, reading Shadow of the Almighty *and* The Journals of Jim Elliot. *The impact of his life was epic in shaping a worldview of missions, and the Lord began a tug on my heart. Education and experience took me down a business track and for years my engagement in "missions" was quiet. Then, as the Lord would have it, I found myself in Ghana for a short-term trip where the most random of relationships began. I was introduced to many challenging philosophies of missions and then specifically to the community of healthcare missions. Soon after that journey I began working with the Global Missions Health Conference and this amazing group of organizations, leaders, and practitioners. This season of life also blended with various global projects which kept my travels international for several years and exposed my mind and heart to a whole world of need and potential.*

The years have taught me that while I used to think missions was something reserved for the Christian elite, now I see missions as a way of life and a framework of your heart. And most of all, I'm continually reminded the Lord is far more interested in holding our heart close than about how we serve Him. Now I know that my work with hundreds of organizations and thousands of individuals for their engagement in missions is how the Lord wants me to live a missional life during this season. The Lord has been good to guide me into the richness of this missions world in ways I never thought possible.

"TELL ME AND I FORGET,
TEACH ME AND I MAY REMEMBER,
INVOLVE ME AND I LEARN." –Benjamin Franklin

Will Rogers began working on changing organizations for purposed strategies while in college, as he served as the president of the student body (SGA) at Milligan College. Following graduation, Will took a leadership position with Focus on the Family working with some of the nation's most talented college leaders in a leadership development program. After the Focus Leadership Institute, Will moved to Florida to serve as the Chief Operating Officer of Christian Financial Services assisting in developing strategy, marketing initiatives, and operational procedures. Opportunities continued in the development of an international internship program for college students through various global partners. In 2006 Will began working with the Global Missions Health Conference and has overseen its redesign, partnership strategies, and launch of the community website. Will works with various other organizations to assist them in building strong paths for execution on a variety of fields, projects, and continents.

"...and what you have heard from me in the presence of many witnesses entrust to faithful men who will be able to teach others also." 2 Timothy 2:2

WHAT TO LOOK FOR IN A MENTOR	THINGS TO ASK OF A MENTOR	WAYS TO ENGAGE A MENTOR
Someone you respect both in professional skill and personal life	How did you get to where you are?	Meet a few times for coffee or a meal
Someone who has walked down a path that interests you	What have you learned along the journey?	Read through a book together
	What would you change or do differently?	If you're participating in a short-term trip, ask someone on the team to meet a few times
	What do you think I should focus my energy on now?	Pray together
		Bring closure at the right time

Resources and References

Books
  Mentoring 101
    by John Maxwell
  Reverse Mentoring
    by Earl Creps

  Mentor Like Jesus
    by Regi Campbell
  Next Generation Leader
    by Andy Stanly

45

CHAPTER 7

IT STARTS LOCALLY

by
Rick Donlon, M.D.

YOU DON'T HAVE TO
FLY OVERSEAS TO
"DO MISSIONS," IT'S RIGHT
IN YOUR BACK YARD

YOU HAVE A
RESPONSIBILITY TO
SERVE THOSE AROUND YOU
JUST AS MUCH AS THOSE
AROUND THE GLOBE.

PERSONAL JOURNEY   Rick Donlon

Early in my second year of medical school, in my hometown of New Orleans, a woman in my Sunday school class asked me to help her start a Saturday morning Bible club in the Fischer Housing Projects. The Fischer Projects are gone now, but in the 1980s they were infamous as one of New Orleans' largest and riskiest public housing developments. On a few late nights in my pre-Christian high school days, I'd driven through Fischer with friends, fueled by beer and a desire for thrills. Otherwise, I'd stayed as far from the area as possible.

That first Saturday morning, a few folks from the church and a handful of medical students formed a tight caravan and drove to the meeting space in the middle of Fischer. It's laughable now, but we were petrified, expecting to be shot at in the first moments. The few young men who approached us were friendly enough; they presumed we were there to purchase cocaine. But the Bible club went well; we came back the next week and many weeks after that. I'd spent time on short-term mission trips overseas, but those experiences in the Fischer Housing Projects were my first extended introduction to local, cross-cultural ministry.

I'm grateful someone challenged me to move outside of my comfort zone, even in the midst of a stressful second year of medical school. Many of us convince ourselves we can't be involved in ministry and spiritual growth during the taxing years of professional school. We reason it's wise stewardship to focus almost exclusively on our studies. After watching medical, dental, and other professional students for two decades, I know just the opposite is true. We must find ways to participate in God's expanding Kingdom at every stage of our preparation, if we expect to maintain our vision and eventually bear fruit.

Recently, our Memphis house churches commissioned a team of three families and a single woman as missionaries to an unreached part of North Africa. They're the fourth team we've sent out in the last decade; the other three are laboring in other parts of North Africa, Central Asia, and North India. Without exception, the members of all four teams learned cross-cultural ministry skills through living, working, and "churching" in the low-income African American neighborhoods where we operate health centers. Many of the challenges of overseas ministry among unreached people groups—danger, limited resources, culture shock—exist in America's poor urban and rural communities. Fruitful ministry for our overseas medical and dental missionaries began with ministry experience among the poor and oppressed in Memphis. Similar opportunities exist in nearly every corner of the US.

Jesus gave us a principle in Luke 16:10: "One who is faithful in a very little is also faithful in much, and one who is dishonest in a very little is also dishonest in much." We've got to faithfully steward our time and talents for the Kingdom of God now, even in the midst of preparation, if we expect to be fruitful later.

HOW TO GET STARTED

READ two life-changing missionary biographies that demonstrate how faithful local service leads to overseas fruitfulness.
William Carey
by his grandson, S. Pearce Carey
To The Golden Shore: The Life Of Adoniram Judson
by Courtney Anderson

FIND OUT what organizations or churches are active in the communities of need in your city or town. *Find a way to work alongside those disciples.*

TAKE AN HONEST INVENTORY of how you spend your time and money now. Are you living faithfully at this time, when you have been given little? If not, make concrete, objective changes.

HOW CAN YOU BECOME more involved in authentic Christian community? Ask God to bring like-minded missional disciples into your life, for the purposes of mutual edification and accountability.

I'm grateful someone challenged me to move outside of my comfort zone, even in the midst of a stressful second year of medical school.

49

"Start by doing what's necessary; then do what's possible; and suddenly you are doing the impossible."

"LOVE BEGINS AT HOME, AND IT IS NOT HOW MUCH WE DO...BUT HOW MUCH LOVE WE PUT IN THAT ACTION" –Mother Teresa

Rick Donlon grew up in New Orleans and graduated from Texas Christian University in 1986. He completed medical school at Louisiana State University, New Orleans, and a combined Internal Medicine and Pediatrics residency at the University of Tennessee, Memphis. In 1995 he and three medical school classmates opened Christ Community Health Services (CCHS), a primary-care health center for the poor in Memphis' most medically underserved neighborhood. Over the last 18 years, CCHS has grown to include six health centers, three dental clinics, and a family medicine residency program. Christ Community's thirty-five full-time physicians, fifteen midlevel practitioners, and six dentists provide over 140,000 patient visits and deliver 700 babies annually. Many of Christ Community's medical and dental providers, including Dr. Donlon, live in the underserved communities where they work. Over the last ten years CCHS has sent long-term medical missionaries to unreached people groups in Central and South Asia and the Horn of Africa. Dr. Donlon serves as Christ Community's Chief Executive Officer and the Clinical Director of HIV/AIDS Services. He and his wife Laurie and their seven children live in the Binghampton neighborhood of Memphis, where he works and serves as an elder in their house church network.

"Let no one despise you for your youth, but set the believers an example in speech, in conduct, in love, in faith, in purity. Do not neglect the gift you have...Practice these things, immerse yourself in them, so that all may see your progress."

1 Timothy 4:12, 14A, 15

CHAPTER 8

SELECTING A
SHORT-TERM
TRIP

by

Don Thompson, M.D.

SUCCESSFULLY FIND AND PARTICIPATE IN A SHORT-TERM TRIP

WITHOUT DAMAGING THOSE WE SERVE.

You have more mission opportunities today than ever before! You can travel halfway around the world, serve for a few days, and still make it home for school or work on Monday morning! With so much available at your doorstep, it is more important than ever to carefully select your short-term trip.

THE 1ST STEP

Do some self-examination as you choose a geographic location and an organization. You should ask yourself the question, **"Why do I want to go?"** An honest, thoughtful time of introspection will help you determine the type of trip to seek and the kind of organization to choose. Some answers to these questions might be to broaden your level of experience in serving others or to give back from your surplus to the needy. Potential spiritual reasons might be learning to share your faith with others from different cultural and faith backgrounds or obeying the Great Commission of our Lord. If the doctrinal stance of the short-term missions group matters to you, then this should also be on your list. Professional reasons might be to participate in a global health experience or to develop cultural intelligence.

THE 2ND STEP

Choose a short-term team by finding an organization whose goals are consistent with your own. Does the group value personal and/or spiritual development while you are serving as a short-term medical missionary? Is their focus on providing healthcare to a particular group of needy people, or do they have other priorities, like evangelism, strengthening local partners, or health education? Or can they do several of these? If you are not a graduate physician, dentist, or nurse, you must find a group that takes students.

AFTER YOU SPEND SOME TIME ON THESE TWO STEPS, develop a short list of organizations you think might match your passion areas and motivations. Ask around—talk to people who have served with the short-term missions organizations you are considering, and learn from their experiences. Don't take their recommendations blindly, though. They may have had different reasons for going than you have, so their experience may be different than what yours could be—for good or bad. Prioritize your list based on these recommendations from others, ask God for His wisdom and direction in choosing the right trip, then *TAKE THE PLUNGE!*

THE
FINAL
STEP
Evaluate your experience after you return. Were your expectations met? If not, were your expectations realistic? Did you learn something new about yourself, about the type of service, or about the short-term organization that you did not know before? Unpack your experiences, spend some time with a mentor who can "fact-check" your expectations and experiences, then do it again!

Most importantly, count on God to reveal to you how and where He wants you to serve Him. The more you depend on Him as you go through this process, the more you will grow in obedience and dependence on Him! Do your homework, and then step out in faith!

I am pretty focused on planning out just about every step of my life! While at times this is a growth area for me, this characteristic has also contributed greatly to my career as a military officer. I have always leaned towards innovation, but I quickly learned innovation is pretty worthless if the good ideas cannot be put into action. Therefore, implementation is key. One of the most valuable lessons I ever learned was from one of my bosses early in my career, who said, "Well, Don, what you see depends on where you sit." I should have learned this lesson in kindergarten, but I must have been sick that day; I usually just tried to push on through the resistance, thinking I knew better.

When I learned to put myself in others' shoes, the resistance to implementing new ideas plummeted! I learned to count the costs, consider the ease of doing new things, and evaluate risks, all from perspectives other than my own. When I started to look at an issue, task, need, or opportunity from another perspective, it became easier to understand the real issues and challenges to implementation.

Why does this matter? Because God provides each of us with a crowd of people who are wired differently than we are. Many of them have had experiences that can benefit us greatly, if we only take the time to ask them and listen to their answers! Successfully choosing a short-term missions opportunity depends on the same deliberate steps. Talk to God. Look at yourself, who you are, and what you (think you) want. Talk to others. Bounce your ideas and thought processes off others. Find a mentor. Be a discipler. Join the community!

"...REMEMBER THE FORMER THINGS OF OLD; FOR I AM GOD, AND THERE IS NO OTHER; I AM GOD, AND THERE IS NONE LIKE ME, DECLARING THE END FROM THE BEGINNING AND FROM ANCIENT TIMES THINGS NOT YET DONE, SAYING, 'MY COUNSEL SHALL STAND, AND I WILL ACCOMPLISH ALL MY PURPOSE,' CALLING A BIRD OF PREY FROM THE EAST, THE MAN OF MY COUNSEL FROM A FAR COUNTRY, I HAVE SPOKEN, AND I WILL BRING IT TO PASS; I HAVE PURPOSED, AND I WILL DO IT."

Isaiah 46:9-11

Dr. Don Thompson serves as the Director of Global Health Outreach, the international mission department of the Christian Medical & Dental Associations. Don attended the F. Edward Hébert School of Medicine in Bethesda, Maryland, and did his family medicine residency training at the Robert L. Thompson Community Hospital in Fort Worth, Texas. He did an additional residency in Preventive Medicine at Tulane University Medical Center in New Orleans, Louisiana, where he also earned a master's degree in Public Health and Tropical Medicine.

> "For from the rising of the sun to its setting my name will be great among the nations, and in every place incense will be offered to my name, and a pure offering. For my name will be great among the nations, says the Lord of hosts."
>
> Malachi 1:11

Why do I want to do short-term missions?

- Adventure
- Serving others
- Giving back to the needy
- Getting international experience
- Working across cultures
- Obeying the Great Commission
- Learning to share my faith

What distinguishes one short-term missions group from another?

- Has experienced, trained, capable team leaders
- Prepares and equips team members prior to the short-term trip
- Groups have healthy, interdependent relationships with national partners rather than being served by them
- Assures debriefing for team members upon return
- Provides skilled, reliable administrative support with integrity

> "And Jesus came and said to them, 'All authority in heaven and on earth has been given to me. Go therefore and make disciples of all nations, baptizing them in the name of the Father and of the Son and of the Holy Spirit, teaching them to observe all that I have commanded you. And behold, I am with you always, to the end of the age.'"
>
> Matthew 28:18-20

Resources and References

Books
   The Call
      by Os Guinness
   Spiritual Depression
      by David Martyn Lloyd-Jones
   Jesus, M.D.
      by David Stevens
   Let the Nations Be Glad
      by John Piper

   Preach and Heal
      by Charles Fielding
   Foreign to Familiar
      by Sarah Lister
   Leading with Cultural Intelligence
      by David Livermore
   Beyond Medicine
      by David Stevens

Website
   www.perspectives.org

NAVIGATING
SENDING
AGENCIES

by
Scott Reichenbach, R.N.

FEELING CONFIDENT
EXPLORING
THE ORGANIZATIONS THAT
CAN SEND YOU LONG-TERM

NAVIGATING SENDING AGENCIES

You sense God has called you to heal the sick and preach the message of salvation as He called the 72 in Luke 10. How do you take the next step of navigating the huge number of sending agencies?

Partnering with a sending agency that understands the complexities of international missions and the unique demands of a healthcare ministry is foundational to serving full-time overseas as a medical missionary. A sending agency is an organization that exists, in partnership with the local church, to prepare and support people called by the Holy Spirit to carry out the Great Commission in other lands. They provide leadership, accountability, community, and the necessary personal and logistical support (visas, insurance, finances, taxes, retirement, security, etc.).

There is not one perfect agency. Each has its own personality. Dr. Thomas Hale, in *On Being a Missionary*, likens finding a sending agency to finding a spouse. As in marriage, selecting an agency requires dialogue between both parties to determine unity and compatibility of mission and vision.

If you know the ministry, location, or people you wish to serve, talk to those missionaries and organizations. Take the opportunity during your training, to serve alongside them to learn how the agency functions on the field level.

Look to your church leadership for agencies that align with or are similar in theology. Keep in mind that your pastor(s) should know you well as ALL agencies will want to hear from your church leaders about your suitability for ministry. If you do not have strong ties to a particular church, develop that relationship now. It is vital to have a sending church that prayerfully supports you in ministry.

Do you have educational debt? Explore Project MedSend's list of associate organizations. Serving with one of their associates will allow you to be eligible to receive MedSend's educational loan repayment grant.

With this narrowing list, begin to build relationships in the organizations, even if it is years before you are ready to serve. Dialogue about their theology, mission, vision, and passion for healthcare ministry, and ask questions (there are many —see questions). Is there agreement? Gain an understanding of their structure, selection, and orientation process and their ability to care for you and your family overseas. Initiating this conversation today will allow you to get to know the agencies and the people involved in the process both in the home office and abroad.

Most sending agencies have years of experience and can provide valuable insight that the Lord may use to guide you. Finding the right sending agency requires prayer and a spirit of humility. God called you to be a part of the work He is doing; seek and trust Him. He may even use the agency to confirm His call or help redirect you to another location or ministry.

—Hudson Taylor

What is the healthcare mission and vision God has called me to?

Who would be my sending church and how well do they know me?

Who are the missionaries and sending agencies I know and respect?

What do I think I would want or need from a sending agency?

QUESTIONS TO ASK AS YOU
NAVIGATE SENDING AGENCIES

What is the history of the agency?

Their history will give you an idea of where the organization was, where they are now, and where they may be going in the future.

How did it originate?

On what principles was it founded?

In what ways have they adjusted to the changing generation?

What is the spiritual makeup of the mission agency?

IT IS IMPORTANT THAT YOU ARE IN AGREEMENT WITH THE FOUNDATIONAL BIBLICAL TENETS OF THE ORGANIZATION

What are their doctrinal statements and core beliefs?

What is their mission statement?

What are their spiritual life policies and standards?

THEIR CORE VALUES AND GOALS WILL INDICATE THEIR DIRECTION FOR MINISTRY

What is their strategy and methodology for missions?

What is their vision? Goals and objectives?

What is their focus? Church planting, discipleship, healthcare?

Is it based on location? e.g., 10/40 window, Africa, etc.

Is it based on people groups? e.g., Muslim ministry

What types of ministries or platforms do they currently support?

Where are their missionaries currently serving?

Are they open to new locations and ministries?

How do they partner with the local church – domestically and internationally?

Do they have an exit strategy or vision for sustainability?

What is the organizational structure of the sending agency?

UNDERSTANDING HOW DECISIONS ARE MADE WILL ALSO INFLUENCE WHO YOU SHOULD TALK TO. IF MOST OF THE DIRECTION COMES FROM FIELD LEADERSHIP, IT IS IMPORTANT TO SPEAK TO THE LEADERS ON THE FIELD WHERE YOU WILL BE SERVING.

How large is the organization? Do they work in teams or are individuals sent?

How are decisions made? Is it centralized, democratic, personalized, home office, or field based?

Who do missionaries report to and how are their goals set? How and how often are they measured?

How much autonomy do you have to make decisions regarding your work on the field?

What are the selection and orientation requirements and process?

What is the application process and how are new missionaries approved?

What pre-field training is required and/or provided?

Specific Bible courses or biblical training?

Cultural training?

Medical training or orientation?

What on-field orientation is provided?

What is their policy on language study?

What are the expectations for first-term missionaries?

FINANCIAL

Do you raise support or is support provided?

What tools do they provide to help you raise support?

WHAT ABOUT BENEFITS AND MISCELLANEOUS EXPENSES— HEALTH, LIFE, DISABILITY, AND EVACUATION INSURANCE, PENSION, VACATION, TAXES, HOUSING, EDUCATION, PERSONAL AND MINISTRY EXPENSES?

How do they provide financial accountability?

Are they a member of Project MedSend?

What does their missionary care and support look like?

SPIRITUAL

Is there ongoing encouragement and opportunities for spiritual growth—while on the field, when home on furlough?

EMOTIONAL

Is there counseling in crisis and debriefing?

FAMILY

What support do they offer for singles or families? Spouse? Vacation time?

SOCIAL

What are the rules for the education of children?

PHYSICAL

What are the medical, retirement, and disability benefits?

Do they provide mentorship, accountability, supervision, discipline?

What is the relationship with US partner churches?

Does the agency have expectations of the sending church?

What are their expectations for your relationship with your sending church(es)?

Do you need to belong to a certain denomination?

How do they utilize medical practitioners (i.e., your specialty)?

SUPPORT FOR YOUR MEDICAL MINISTRY AND UNITY IN VISION IS KEY

What is their vision for healthcare ministry?

What is their experience in healthcare ministry?

How many of their missionaries are medical?

Do they have personnel in the home office that understand the needs and challenges of medical missions?

What are their expectations for you as a medical professional?

What about continuing medical education requirements?

Are you allowed to work within your profession while on furlough?

What is their idea of sustainability in medical missions?

What about the role of nationals in the healthcare setting?

My journey to a missional life has been a process of maturing faith, drawing closer to the Lord through His Word and through opportunities to serve Him. I have learned that the God of creation, the God of the Old and New Testament, is my Savior and friend!

I entered pediatric nursing with the goal of ministering to the physical and spiritual needs of patients. In His time He provided opportunities to serve. In those situations I learned more about myself and grew in my relationship with the Lord more than I provided any service or ministry to others. Sitting with patients in remote Mozambique and North Sudan, where the needs far exceeded our medical resources, my faith and understanding of God was both challenged and deepened. Living the missional life is a matter of obedience and trust. Do I trust the Lord with my life, my family, the situation? Is He truly Lord of my life?

While working at Samaritan's Purse, I was privileged to help launch over 90 young physicians who, when called by the Lord, obeyed and went. In my heart, I wanted to be the one going; however, the Lord chose to use me in ways I did not expect. But through their obedience and trust I witnessed the tremendous ripple effect of a missional life.

As I continue on this journey my prayer is that of Paul's in Colossians 4; that I may devote myself to prayer, being watchful and thankful; making the most of every opportunity, praying for open doors for the message, so that I may proclaim clearly the mystery of Christ.

"SEND ME ANYWHERE, ONLY GO WITH ME. LAY ANY BURDEN ON ME, ONLY SUSTAIN ME. SEVER ANY TIE, BUT THE TIES THAT BIND ME TO YOUR SERVICE AND TO YOUR HEART."

—David Livingstone

After 11 years of pediatric critical care nursing, Scott joined Samaritan's Purse to coordinate the Post-Residency Program which he led for seven years. Scott holds a BSN from Messiah College and recently returned to nursing in the post-anesthesia care unit. He has remained involved in medical missions by volunteering with the Christian Medical and Dental Association and Christian Health Service Corps. Scott has served short-term in Honduras, Mozambique, and Sudan and has visited mission hospitals and clinics around the world. Scott lives in Boone, NC with his wife, Rachel, their three children, and nine chickens.

"The spirit of Christ is the spirit of missions. The nearer we get to Him, the more intensely missionary we become."

—Henry Martyn

Resources and References

Books

Ask a Missionary
  by John McVay
Global Mission Handbook
  by Steve Hoke and Bill Taylor
Mission Handbook: US and Canadian Protestant Ministries Overseas 21st Edition
  by Linda J. Weber

On Being a Missionary
  by Thomas Hale
Shadow of the Almighty: The Life and Testament of Jim Elliot
  by Elisabeth Elliot

Websites

www.medicalmissions.com/network
www.askamissionary.com/topic/mission-agencies
www.medsend.org

BUILDING A
FINANCIAL
PLAN

by
Rick Allen

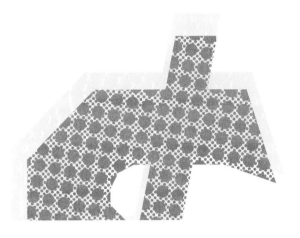

BE CONFIDENT THAT YOU CAN OVERCOME THE
COMPLEXITIES OF RAISING FUNDS FOR MISSIONS.

"For from him and through him and to him are all things. To him be glory forever. Amen."
Romans 11:36

If God has called you to be a healthcare missionary, you are about to experience one of the most satisfying – and challenging – careers in the world.

You will be a warrior for God in a hostile land. Like any soldier, you need a time of preparation – what the military refers to as "boot camp" – and that time should begin now, before you enter your mission field. An important goal of boot camp is to develop or reinforce lifestyle disciplines. As a healthcare missionary, those disciplines include daily Bible reading, prayer, fasting, serving others, and financial stewardship or money management.

You may not have thought of financial stewardship as a spiritual discipline before, but it is an element of spiritual maturity that affects all aspects of Christian life. As a Christ follower, you should consider all your resources to be owned by the Lord. He may allow you to possess or use material things, but ultimately all things belong to Him.

You should also realize that serving and giving can be hindered by financial debt. Debt of any kind commits you to someone else. Left unchecked, significant debt can influence or even control your decisions. Yet you may be among the many healthcare professionals who must borrow significant amounts of money in order to complete their studies. If so, we want to encourage you to remain as debt-free as possible so you can serve God unencumbered.

Before taking any loans, develop and adhere to a financial control plan. Begin with a fairly accurate estimate of how much income you will have available from your student loan account, other income, or savings. Then approximate how much it will cost you to live, based on your recent history adjusted to your current situation. Decide how you will disburse your income, considering what percentages will go to tithing, taxes, debt repayment, living expenses and necessities, savings, and lifestyle.

As you pursue your education, borrow the minimum amount necessary and use that money only to meet your most basic needs. Although some may encourage you to live lavishly, if you believe God has called you to be a healthcare missionary you should begin developing a missionary mindset now. Missionaries use things up, wear things out, make things do, or do without. God wants you to learn to be content with what He has provided, not beholden to the things of this world.

It won't be easy. You will need great faith and trust to submit to God's direction in managing your material resources. But be assured that when the Lord called you into healthcare ministry, He had already made a way for you to follow Him. For many healthcare missionaries, MedSend's educational loan repayment grants are part of that plan. But whether or not MedSend is in your future, one thing is certain: the challenges of practicing financial stewardship as a spiritual discipline will be greatly outweighed by the freedom, joy, and blessings that will result!

After 25 years building a career in the business world, the Lord called me into full-time ministry as a pastor and missions leader. When God called, my family and I had to make significant changes. We were living a lifestyle reflective of the choices I had made up to that time. In order to respond to God's call, we needed to make painful decisions – which could have been avoided had I planned better to allow God to use me. Through His grace to me and my family, I was able to eliminate all debt, freeing us to serve as our Lord led. As I look back, I realize I could have missed the blessings the Lord had in store for me and my family because of the financial choices I made earlier in life.

"OWE NO ONE ANYTHING, EXCEPT TO LOVE EACH OTHER, FOR THE ONE WHO LOVES ANOTHER HAS FULFILLED THE LAW." Romans 13:8

Rick brings an extensive background in business and ministry to his role as MedSend's president. With a degree in finance and marketing from Temple University, he spent 25 years as a corporate executive, where he was instrumental in the rapid growth and turnaround of several high-tech businesses. Rick and his wife Linda have four daughters and live in Connecticut where he also serves as Campus Pastor of a multi-site church.

Resources and References

Books
Cost Effective College: Creative Ways to Pay for College and Stay Out of Debt
by Gordon Wadsworth

Websites
Crown Financial Ministries
www.crown.org

START LIVING A
MISSIONARY LIFESTYLE

IT IS NEVER TOO EARLY TO START LIVING
A "MISSIONARY LIFESTYLE." BY THAT WE MEAN:

MISSIONARIES...

...buy what they need, not what they want. They want what they have. Missionaries can't afford everything they want, but they can afford what they need.

...use things up, wear things out, make things do, or do without.

...have a conserver mentality rather than a consumer mentality.

...don't "shop." They buy with a list of needs and don't buy anything by impulse. Shopping leads to buying things you don't really need.

...always maintain the spiritual discipline of giving to God, but not with borrowed money. Sometimes they can only give by self-denial – giving up a necessity in order to give to God.

DEMONSTRATE
FINANCIAL STEWARDSHIP

THE LESS YOU BORROW, THE EASIER IT WILL BE
FOR YOU TO ENTER FULL-TIME CHRISTIAN SERVICE AND LEAD A VICTORIOUS CHRISTIAN LIFE.
YOU CAN DEVELOP HABITS THAT INSURE A LIFETIME OF FINANCIAL SUCCESS REGARDLESS OF
HOW MUCH INCOME YOU EARN. SOME TIPS:

Borrow with great care, for needs only and with a budget in hand. Typically, a person with a restrained lifestyle can live on thousands less than lenders recommend.

To minimize educational borrowing, it often makes sense to attend the least expensive US school you can, which is usually your state university. A conscientious student can get an excellent education in any licensed, reputable program. Always think about repayment.

Begin making loan payments even before required – as soon as you earn your first dollar.

Do not use borrowed money for short-term missions trips.

If you have educational debt, we recommend limiting tithing to 10% and not supporting other missionaries. Focus instead on debt reduction.

Only use credit cards when absolutely necessary and never for long-term financing.

Do not make financial investments while in debt, except for employer-paid pensions, IRAs and other tax saving or deferring investments.

Trust the Lord
to provide at
every junction
along your path.

71

CHAPTER

11

OVERCOMING CHALLENGES
TO MISSIONS

by
David Stevens, M.D.

KNOWING THE
LORD IS GREATER THAN

**ANY CHALLENGE THAT
WOULD PREVENT YOU**

FROM ENTERING
MISSIONS

❰ YOU'VE UPSET THE DEVIL! ❱

HE DETESTS YOU OBEYING THE GREAT COMMISSION AND BECOMING A MEDICAL MISSIONARY BECAUSE HE KNOWS GOD CAN USE YOU TO BRING HEALING AND SALVATION TO MULTITUDES OF PEOPLE. HE WILL GO OUT OF HIS WAY TO ENHANCE YOUR FEARS AND THROW OBSTACLES IN YOUR PATH WITH THE GOAL OF DISCOURAGING, DELAYING, OR EVEN DEFEATING YOUR JOURNEY INTO MISSIONS.

BUT I'VE GOT GOOD NEWS! **THOUSANDS OF MISSIONARIES HAVE TRAVELED THIS SAME PATH SUCCESSFULLY AND HAVE OVERCOME EVERY OBSTRUCTION. WITH PERSEVERANCE AND FORESIGHT, YOU CAN TOO!** *HERE IS WHAT TO WATCH OUT FOR AND TIPS FOR DEALING WITH EACH DIFFICULTY.*

FUNDRAISING

Denominations often draw your support from pooled funds, but most missionaries serve with "faith-based" organizations that require them to raise their support. *Relax and realize it gives you the opportunity to have as much ministry in the US as overseas.* There has never been a medical missionary who has failed in raising support. Your mission will train you and many people will be eager for you to be "their missionaries" and provide the prayer and financial support you need.

MARRIAGE

The most common reason those called don't go is they marry someone who is not called. If a potential mate is not called to missions, don't date them. It may not be God's will that you marry that person.

Obstacles will come your way, but God, if you allow Him, can conquer each one.

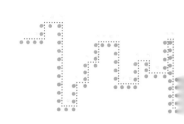

CHILDREN

Our biggest fear was taking our children overseas. Our biggest fear when God called us to return to the US was bringing them back! The mission field is a wonderful place to raise children. The US is the dangerous jungle. You will have closer relationships, more mature children, and a multitude of missionary "aunts" and "uncles." In addition, studies show that missionary kids are among the highest achievers. The biggest sacrifice is being far from your extended family, but God is sufficient and overseas travel is cheap!

SINGLENESS

Half or more missionaries are single like Paul, so don't delay going because you are going alone. The best place to find someone who shares your passion for ministry is on the mission field!

FEAR

Fear of change, burnout, incompetence, language learning, a new culture, strange foods, personal safety, and dozens of other things can paralyze you if you let them. God hasn't called you to what He didn't design you to do. He promises that His grace is sufficient and that He will go with you every step of the way. The closer you get to Him through prayer, meditation, and Bible study, the more confidence you will have in His sufficiency.

FAMILY SUPPORT

I hope your family loves God enough to release you and support you in His service, but this may not be true for you. *As a Christian adult, your allegiance to God supersedes your responsibility to your parents. Love and honor them, but follow God's call. Your faithful life may draw them closer to Christ.*

As you follow Him, He will work in you and through you to change the world.

What a journey!!

Most of my friends had never been in an airplane when my dad took me to Haiti on a mission trip during my freshman year of high school in 1966. I saw a nurse diagnosing, treating and leading people to Christ, and God used that need and my science aptitude to call me into medical missions as I sought His will. During my freshman year at Asbury University, I surrendered my will completely to Him. The summer of my junior year my dad encouraged me to work with Dr. Ernie Steury at Tenwek Hospital in Kenya. I delivered my first baby, assisted in surgery, and was mentored by Ernie each day. I came back home knowing God was calling me to Tenwek and went under preliminary appointment with World Gospel Mission.

I was dating my future wife Jody and God put the same call in her heart. We were married after my first year of medical school and went back to Tenwek later for an eight-week rotation together. Less than a year after residency, we were career missionaries. I loved the wide scope of missionary medicine and helped expand the hospital from 135 to 300 beds, start a community health program, build a hydroelectric plant, develop a nursing school, and start a chaplaincy training center.

It was easy following God's call to Africa but difficult when He called us back to the States 11 years later. I thought it was to help other mission hospitals as the medical director of Samaritan's Purse, but that was only part of His plan. Soon I was leading relief teams into wars and disasters in Somalia, Sudan, Bosnia, and Rwanda.

In 1994, God called us evangelize, disciple, and mobilize doctors to ministry and missions through the Christian Medical & Dental Associations. He has done that more than we could have ever imagined!

"IF THE GREAT COMMISSION IS TRUE, OUR PLANS ARE NOT TOO BIG; THEY ARE TOO SMALL."

—Pat Morley

Dr. David Stevens is the Chief Executive Officer of the Christian Medical & Dental Associations (CMDA), the nation's largest faith-based organization of doctors. As spokesman for more than 17,000 doctors, Dr. Stevens has conducted hundreds of media interviews. Prior to his service with CMDA, he served as medical director of Samaritan's Purse. From 1985 to 1991, Dr. Stevens served as executive officer and medical superintendent of Tenwek Hospital in Bomet, Kenya. He helped to transform Tenwek Hospital into one of the premier mission healthcare facilities in that country.

≫ **FAN THE FLAME.** ≪

≫ Surrender completely to God's will. ≪

≫ *KEEP SURRENDERING.* ≪

≫ **READ MEDICAL MISSION BOOKS.** ≪

≫ Attend a mission-minded church. ≪

≫ Develop a relationship with a medical missionary. ≪

≫ ≪

≫ Avoid marrying someone not called to missions. ≪

≫ **ATTEND MISSION CONFERENCES REGULARLY.** ≪

≫ *Do rotations or mission trips overseas during training.* ≪

≫ **Explore mission agencies through medicalmissions.com.** ≪

≫ SEEK ADVICE AND GOD'S GUIDANCE ON YOUR TRAINING PATH. ≪

≫ MINIMIZE YOUR FINANCIAL AND POSSESSION ENTANGLEMENTS. ≪

≫ **DELAY IS DEADLY. AFTER TRAINING, GET TO THE MISSION FIELD!** ≪

Resources and References

Books
Beyond Medicine: What Else You Need To Know
To Be a Healthcare Missionary
  by David Stevens, M.D.
On Being a Missionary
  by Tom Hale, M.D.
Jesus, M.D.
  by David Stevens, M.D.
Miracle at Tenwek
  by Gregg Lewis
Handbook of Medicine in Developing Countries
  by Dennis Palmer, D.O. and Catherine E. Wolf, M.D.

Websites
www.cmda.org

Podcasts (available at medicalmissions.com)
  A Missionary Life—Is It For You?
  Interview With the Legendary Missionary
    Dr. Paul Brand
  Interview With Pioneer Medical
    Missionary Dr. Ernie Steury

CHAPTER

12

UNDERSTANDING CURRENT
HEALTHCARE
NEEDS

by
Clydette Powell, M.D., M.P.H., F.A.A.P.

KNOW HOW TO WALK EFFECTIVELY
—NOT FOOLISHLY—
IN THE WORLD OF HEALTHCARE MISSIONS TODAY.

A THOUGHTFUL EXAMINATION OF OTHERS' HEALTHCARE NEEDS, WHETHER THOSE OF AN INDIVIDUAL, A COMMUNITY, OR EVEN A COUNTRY, PLACES YOU IN A BETTER POSITION TO SERVE THEIR NEEDS, RATHER THAN YOUR OWN.

Understanding real and perceived healthcare needs is more likely to lead to a clear mission, well-articulated goals and objectives, and robust measures of outcome and impact. As a result, you will work more effectively alongside those you want to serve. This principle applies no matter what the location, size, timing, or duration of an activity, project, or program. So, how do you begin to understand this before undertaking a project or a mission in healthcare?

For long-term domestic and global public health missions, you should grasp the major health challenges and trends, local/global initiatives and implementing partners, and the history of setbacks and successes in the area you want to serve. This "situational assessment" can seem a big task, but it merits the investment of your time and energy. The effort will help to avoid frustration, mismatched expectations on your part and theirs, and poor stewardship of human and financial resources. It's important to understand the larger context of your work even in short-term missions, as it may facilitate or hamper the work of your predecessors or those who will follow up after you leave.

Having some sense of your geographic focus and target population can help you select the essential facts out of what can seem like an endless source of information (and misinformation). Search for core information such as the population pyramid, the causes of morbidity and mortality, the political will of the local authorities, the budgetary support, and the competing priorities from other health and non-health sectors, to name a few. You also need to know who is already working there.

Find out where major donors, national and international agencies, and partners are placing their emphasis. Websites will reveal their country and programmatic priorities as well as their expertise. For example, take a look at websites for the US Agency for International Development (USAID), the US Centers for Disease Control and Prevention (CDC), various UN organizations (e.g., WHO, UNFPA, UNDP, IOM), The Bill and Melinda Gates Foundation, and the Global Fund to Fight AIDS, TB and Malaria. In addition, non-governmental organizations (NGO), health professional associations, private and charitable foundations, and grant-making institutions have their own websites which explain their aims and activities. These websites may have free downloadable documents, issues papers, research studies, and current event video clips and press releases.

In addition to researching these sources, seek out people who are regarded as "subject matter experts" and have direct field experience. Those who work at central levels within Ministries of Health, other government agencies, or with donors and headquarters of implementing partners, have valuable programmatic insights that may not be covered in formal documents or web-based reports. Those who work at the periphery (e.g., community-based level) have on-the-ground experience and information that can be practical for your planning purposes.

TURN DATA INTO INFORMATION:

Health data and information come from many sources. Selected resources are listed on page 85. Demographic and Health Surveys as well as Population Reference Bureau reports provide well-researched profiles of developing countries' health status. The World Bank, UN organizations such as UNICEF and the World Health Organization (WHO), and other institutions publish annual country-level reports. Within those organizations are special focus areas such as infectious diseases, maternal and child health, family planning, nutrition, environmental health, laboratory services, essential drugs, and disaster relief, as well as cross-cutting areas such as health systems strengthening, health care financing, and gender equality. The CDC produces online Morbidity and Mortality Weekly Reports (MMWR) which contain surveillance data as well as descriptive and analytical reports on many aspects of US health status and trends. The US Bureau of the Census and US state/county health departments share data on the healthcare needs of their constituents; sometimes data can even be obtained at zip code level.

Lastly, keep in mind that healthcare issues do not exist in isolation. The health sector intersects with education, agriculture, commerce/economic growth and trade/labor, climate change, democracy and governance, food security, human rights and justice. Those realities can have significant impact on health status and needs. Moreover, these can drastically shift when natural and human-made disasters occur. Conflict-affected areas will have different healthcare priorities than places where peace allows for sustainable development.

"I don't do big things:
I do small things
with big love." —Mother Teresa

I grew up bi-culturally, with a Brazilian mother and American father. Because my father served in the US Navy, we lived overseas periodically. I attended high school while we were living abroad and discovered in my high school years that my calling was in medicine. When I put my hand to that plow, I never looked back and am grateful for that calling, choice, and privilege of service. Discovering that a career in public health work would allow me to help communities and countries, as well as the individuals in them, was a later epiphany. I love clinical medicine and still practice as a child neurologist, and I deeply appreciate the opportunity to forge professional friendships and be engaged in long-term programs that improve the health of populations in developing countries. My formal work with USAID began in 2001, shortly after I discovered that my Brazilian grandfather died of TB in the 1920s, long before the era of anti-TB medications. That revelation reset my course in public health, and God provided the timely employment venue at USAID/Washington for me to take on the challenges of combating a disease that has existed for thousands of years.

Years before I started my current job, I had the opportunity to work as a medical missionary in Cambodia for two years. I reflected many months about that option, as it meant leaving academic medicine and leaving my parents back in the States. However, after long reflection and prayer, I decided to make that change; it turned out to be one of the most significant and positive decisions in my life. Years later, I still reflect on all that God taught me—and my family—in those circumstances, and how much I grew professionally as well. I am grateful.

Dr Clydette Powell works as a Medical Officer for the US Agency for International Development in Washington, DC. She focuses on global tuberculosis programs – in Asia, Africa, and Latin America—with a special emphasis on child TB. She graduated from the Johns Hopkins School of Medicine and holds a Master's degree in Public Health (epidemiology) from University of California at Los Angeles. She received her training in pediatrics and child neurology at the University of Pittsburgh Hospitals and Clinics and Children's Hospital of Pittsburgh. She is triple board certified in pediatrics, child neurology, and preventive medicine/public health. She holds a faculty position as Associate Professor of Pediatrics at The George Washington University School of Medicine in Washington, DC. One of her other interests is the intersection of health and human trafficking; she has written, given presentations, provided services to victims, and worked as an advocate in a local and global context. For two years in the 1980s she served as a medical missionary in Cambodia with World Vision, and she has done short-term missions work in Democratic Republic of the Congo (Zaire), Haiti, Nicaragua, Chile, Albania, and Kosova. She has received a number of awards, including the Woodrow Wilson Award for Distinguished Government Service. Dr. Powell's native language is English, and she has skills in French, Portuguese, Spanish, and basic Cambodian.

"But seek first the kingdom of God and his righteousness, and all these things will be added to you."

Matthew 6:33

Resources and References

Books

Essentials of Global Health
  by R. Skolnik
Understanding Global Health
  by WH Markle, MA Fisher, RA Smego, eds.

American Academy of Pediatrics Textbook
of Global Child Health
  by DM Kamat, PR Fischer

Explore websites, documents, publications from:

US government agencies:
USAID, CDC, NIH, HHS, HRSA, DOS/OGAC
Donor Agencies:
  USAID, CIDA, World Bank, JICA, DFLD
Private foundations:
  The Bill and Melinda Gates Foundation,
  Templeton Foundation; Aga Khan Foundation
UN agencies:
  WHO, UNICEF, UNAIDS, UNFPA, IOM, UNDP
Professional Associations:
  American Society of Tropical Medicine and
  Hygiene, American Public Health Association,
  Infectious Disease Society of America, American
  Academy of Pediatrics
Academic centers:
  Consortium for Universities for Global Health
  Universities; professional schools and institutions

Research groups: CHERG (Child Health Epidemiology
  Research Group); Population Reference
  Bureau; MACRO DHS; CORE Group
Private think tanks:
  The Center for Global Development,
  The Kaiser Family Foundation
Faith-based organizations:
  see Christian Connections for International Health
  for a list of member organizations
NGOs: Medecins Sans Frontieres; Oxfam;
  International Federation of the Red Cross and Red
  Crescent Societies; World Vision, World Relief, World
  Concern, World Hope; Project Hope; CARE, Save the
  Children; Samaritan's Purse, World Medical Mission
Other publications: The Lancet; WHO Bulletin;
  CDC's MMWR; Countdown to 2015 Decade
  Report (The Millennium Development Goals);
  American Journal of Disaster Medicine

QUESTIONS/POINTS TO CONSIDER:

Remember that it is not so much what you are doing, but rather for Whom you are doing this work.

In identifying an activity or project, look for an approach that can have a long-lasting impact and the potential to transform. Does the approach promote equity, quality, and access to health care? Will disadvantaged and vulnerable populations benefit from the interventions you design?

Ask yourself if your skill set and prior experience align with the tasks and the needs. Be honest in that assessment.

Identify ways to evaluate and monitor your project. Ask yourself if the work will alleviate suffering and address inequities in healthcare. How will you measure outcome and impact?

Sometimes what is "trending" may not be sustainable or in the best interests of the people you want to serve. Be evidence-based and seek out facts. Do some "ground-truthing" before you jump in.

Look for synergies with non-health sector activities and programs. Are there ways to integrate your project with initiatives which, for example, promote access to education, create new jobs, or improve agricultural and business practices?

CHAPTER 13

THE FUTURE OF
MISSIONS

by
Gil Odendaal, Ph.D., D.Min.

TRENDS AND SHIFTS

CASTING A VISION FOR WHERE THINGS ARE
HEADING IN THE WORLD OF MISSIONS

CURRENT TRENDS AND SHIFTS IN MISSIONS

The missiological landscape has been changing at a breathtaking speed, fueled by globalization in its many facets, the technological revolution, secularism, the rediscovery of holistic ministry (better identified as integral mission), and above all, the awakening Church reclaiming her legitimate role in seeing the Great Commission fulfilled. All of these factors, accompanied by a myriad of related issues, are forcing mission agencies to reposition themselves in this post-post-colonial era, or become obsolete. (Engel and Dryness in *Changing the Mind of Missions: Where Have We Gone Wrong?* page 143 ff.)

The "new wine" God is making needs new wineskins, and it seems the sending agency of the future will be a hybrid between a traditional mission agency and some expression of the local church. No longer willing to just sit at the sidelines and provide funding and prayers, churches are turning from being spectators into being participants and from being consumers into being contributors. This healthy biblical trend also has some serious challenges since zealous Christ followers often lack adequate cultural competencies and experience. They often do not have the ability to provide member care for a growing army of ordinary people, many of them medical professionals, who are burdened to serve the vulnerable around the globe with love and compassion.

The new wine is also a renewed commitment to integral mission, and an embrace of both the Great Commission (Matthew 28) and the Great Commandment (Matthew 22). Rather than doing the physical and spiritual work next to each other, there has been an awakening that word and deed must be seamlessly integrated so that in the words of the Micah Declaration, it is not simply that evangelism and social involvement are to be done alongside each other. Rather, our proclamation has social consequences as we call people to love and repentance in all areas of life. And our social involvement has evangelistic consequences as we bear witness to the transforming grace of Jesus Christ.

THREE OF THESE SHIFTS ARE:

FROM INFORMATION SCARCITY TO INFORMATION ABUNDANCE. Any organization founded before 1990 was founded in an information scarcity environment and all foundational assumptions that shaped its structures and systems reflected that reality. Likewise the utility of their services for students seeking places or ways to serve in medical missions may be limited or irrelevant.

FROM A CLOSED SYSTEM TO AN OPEN SYSTEM. In the new environment where stakeholders on every level expect to help shape and co-create the future, organizations or individuals who cannot embrace this truth will become irrelevant.

FROM HARD POWER TO SOFT POWER. Hard power is defined as controlling information, agenda, and resources. Soft power, on the other hand, focuses on engagement over exclusion, influence over control. The only credible path to influence is soft power, which is an entirely new skill set for Great Commission influencers from North American churches and mission organizations. But globalization demands it and a Christ-like attitude makes it possible.

THERE ARE ALSO FOUR DICHOTOMIES THAT RENE PADILLA IDENTIFIED THAT HAVE HAD A NEGATIVE IMPACT ON THE MISSION OF THE CHURCH AND THAT ARE SLOWLY CHANGING:

THE DICHOTOMY BETWEEN churches that send out missionaries (generally located in the Christian West) and churches that receive missionaries (almost exclusively in the countries of the so-called two-thirds World: Asia, Africa, and Latin America). Transcultural missions—missions from everywhere to everywhere—is changing this.

THE DICHOTOMY BETWEEN home, located in some country in the Christian West, and the mission field, located in some "pagan" country.

THE DICHOTOMY BETWEEN missionaries called by God to serve Him and common ordinary Christians who enjoy the benefits of salvation but are exempt from sharing in what God wants to do in the world. The priesthood of all believers is effectively emasculated through this position.

THE DICHOTOMY BETWEEN the life and the mission of the church. The same activities supported "overseas" must also be implemented in the local surroundings. The missionary of the 21st century will be someone who is also able to inspire and help the church at "home" to engage in the Great Commission and Great Commandment.

Books

The Meeting of the Waters
by Fritz Kling

Seize the Vuja De
by Steven Moore

The Mission of God's People
by Christopher J. H. Wright

The Radical Disciple
by John Stott

What is Integral Mission
by C. Rene Padilla

Walking with the Poor
by Bryant Myers

The Goal of International Development
by Beth Snodderly

Transforming Worldviews
by Paul G. Hiebert

The Gospel in Human Contexts
by Paul G. Hiebert

Anthropological Reflections on Missiological Issues
by Paul G. Hiebert

Principles of Excellence in Integral Mission
by The Accord Network

A Time for Mission
by Samuel Escobar

What Makes Christian Development Christian
by Tim Chester

Ethics of Evangelism
by Elmer John Thiessen

Mission Between the Times
C. René Padilla

The State of God's World: Globalization and
the Future of Integral Mission
by T. Sine & C. Sine

Going Global
by Lindenberg & Bryant

"NEITHER IS NEW WINE PUT INTO OLD WINESKINS. IF IT IS, THE SKINS BURST AND THE WINE IS SPILLED AND THE SKINS ARE DESTROYED. BUT NEW WINE IS PUT INTO FRESH WINESKINS, AND SO BOTH ARE PRESERVED."

Matthew 9:17

Gil Odendaal, Ph.D., D.Min., is Vice President of Integral Mission at World Relief. From directing global initiatives for Saddleback Church to building innovative programs for other reputable global ministries, Gil has dedicated more than 30 years to empowering the church around the world to seamlessly integrate word and deed ministries that transform communities. He currently spends his time at World Relief innovating ways to empower the church to serve the most vulnerable in both the Global South and North. Whether that church consists of two Christ-followers gathering in a basement in a restricted access country or a church of 20,000 in an open Christian country—the goal is the same—to serve them so that their gospel proclamation has social consequences as they call people to love and repentance in all areas of life. And their social involvement has evangelistic consequences as they bear witness to the transforming grace of Jesus Christ. He regularly speaks and lectures on this topic in the USA and in global settings. Prior to holding his present position, he served as Global Director for PEACE Implementation with Saddleback Church in Lake Forest, California and as Global Director for the HIV/AIDS Initiative under Kay Warren assisting and facilitating the deployment of more than 10,000 short-term missionaries. Other professional positions held by Gil include Regional Coordinator for Africa with Medical Ambassadors International. He also served as Regional Coordinator for Russia and Eastern Europe for a period of two years.

Gil and his wife, Elmarie, were born and raised in South Africa. They have been married for 38 years. They have three adult children and four grandchildren.

UNLESS THESE GLOBAL SHIFTS AND DICHOTOMIES ARE ADDRESSED AND STRUCTURES ARE DESIGNED TO BE NEW WINESKINS THAT CAN CONTAIN THE NEW WINE GOD HAS BEEN MAKING, THE FRUIT OF THE WORK OF A NEW GENERATION OF CHRIST FOLLOWERS MAY "RUN OUT" WHILE ALSO RUINING CURRENT OUTDATED WINESKINS. WHEN WIDELY-HELD ASSUMPTIONS ABOUT HOW WE DO SOMETHING GO UNCHALLENGED, THEY BECOME TRADITIONS. THE NEW GENERATION OF MEDICAL MISSIONARIES MUST BE WILLING TO LOOK AT NEW WAYS OF "DOING MISSIONS," OR WE WILL CONTINUE TO DEFEND UNDERPERFORMING STRUCTURES AND RESIST POTENTIALLY BREAKTHROUGH IDEAS.

PRAYING THROUGH
MISSIONS
PREPARATION

by
Geneva Oaks, Ph.D., R.N.

PRAYER IS

IMPERATIVE IN LIVING OUT A MISSIONAL LIFE.

Scripture teaches us to "pray without ceasing" (1 Thessalonians 5:17). Evangelist C.H. Spurgeon posed questions in response to this command:

What do these words imply?
What do they mean?
How shall we obey them?
Why should we especially obey them?

The questions provide a framework to consider in living a missional life for Jesus Christ.

IMPLICATION: PRAY WITHOUT CEASING

We are never to be in a place where we cannot pray without ceasing. "Every place is hallowed ground to a hallowed heart, and every day is a holy day to a holy man." To pray continually infers a loving conversation between two best friends happening anytime and everywhere.

MEANING: PRAY WITHOUT CEASING

Prayer is a privilege and a precept; an instruction in obedience. As a privilege, we have permission to approach the mercy seat of Christ. We possess sweet permission to pour out our hearts at all times before the Lord. As a precept we are never to abandon prayer; never for any cause or for any reason. "Prayer is a method of worship; continue, therefore, always to render to your Creator, your

Preserver, your Redeemer, your Father, the homage of your prayers." In worship, God must be first and He must be all. The sooner we learn to forget ourselves and to glorify God, the richer the blessing that prayer will bring. "No one ever loses by what he sacrifices for the Father."

OBEDIENCE: THE OF PRAY WITHOUT CEASING

Though prayer is so simple a child can pray, it is the highest and holiest work to which a man can rise. Solomon warns not to rush into God's presence with words, but to sit quietly in awe of our Creator and be willing to pray until God reveals His will.

OBEDIENCE: THE OF PRAY WITHOUT CEASING

We obey because the command to "pray without ceasing" is of divine authority, and because the Lord never ceases to love you, never ceases to bless you, and never ceases to regard you as his child. Pray! for you want a blessing on all the work you are doing. "Unless the Lord builds the house, those who build it labor in vain." (Psalm 127:1) You do not need to fear any circumstance. Pray that at all times you may be fervent, frequent, instant, and constant in prayer; praying in spirit and truth, and always in the name of Jesus Christ.

A MISSIONAL LIFE REQUIRES CONSTANT PRAYER.

I came to know the importance of constant prayer many years after I had committed my life to Christ. I continuously strive to comprehend the enormous sacrificial love of Christ; that while I was still a sinner He chose to die for me. To pray without ceasing is to remain in constant conversation and divine fellowship with the King of Kings and the Lord of Lords and my best friend. It is a privilege too wonderful for me to fathom. I rejoice knowing that God is ever present. He is in my comings and goings. He loves me just as I am. The love I possess as a follower of Christ sustains my desire to live a missional life; a life set apart for God's kingdom work.

It has only been in the past few years that I have had the opportunity to boldly pursue what it means to live missionally. The Lord has provided multiple opportunities for me to journey across the globe in His name. I have been placed in positions of leadership in order to encourage others in their pursuit to live missionally for God's kingdom. I am striving to be obedient to pray without ceasing and to heeding the will of the Lord. I pray the Lord will continue to use me for His kingdom work among the nations and with the people I have the privilege of serving. My desire is for every follower of Christ to come to know the meaning of the Great Commission and a missional life, "following wherever and however the Lord leads." May our lives be "marked by deep commitment and obedience governed by a close relationship with Christ to closely listen, continually hear, and follow through."

Dr. Geneva G. Oaks (G.G.) graduated from Azusa Pacific University School of Nursing and holds a Ph.D. degree in nursing. She is a registered nurse possessing an Advanced Practice degree as a Family Nurse Practitioner. Her primary focus for the profession of nursing lies within the field of Maternal/Child Health. She currently serves as the Dean of California Baptist University School of Nursing. Geneva resides in Jurupa Valley, CA with her husband Donald. They have eight grown children; 16 grandchildren, and one great-grandchild.

Resources and References

Books
Crazy Love: Overwhelmed by a Relentless God
  by Francis Chan
Lord, Teach Us to Pray
  by Andrew Murray

A Passion for Prayer: Experiencing Deeper
Intimacy with God
  by Tom Eliff